TRADITIONAL RC
COMPLINE

ACCORDING TO THE
ROMAN BREVIARY OF 1568

WITH MUSICAL NOTATION BASED ON THE
ROMAN ANTIPHONAL OF 1912

and English translation.

**Canticum
Salomonis**

U. I. O. G. D.

Dear reader, if this book is of profit to you, of your charity offer a prayer for Gerhard Eger, who compiled it, and for Zachary Thomas, without whose help and encouragement it would have never been completed.

Secunda editio, accurate emendata.
Anno reparatæ salutis MMXXI.
© Gerhard Eger. Omnia jura nostra vindicabimus.
Sumptibus & typis «Canticum Salomonis».
sicutincensum.wordpress.com.
ISBN 979-8-4931-9866-3.

Contents.

Proëm 5

Ceremonial Notes 6

Prayers before and after the Divine Office 9

Lord's Prayer, Angelic Salutation, & Symbol 11

Office of Compline 13

Anthems of the Blessed Virgin Mary 38

Aspersion of Holy Water 48

Seasonal and Proper Festal Melodies of the Hymn 50

On Maundy Thursday and Good Friday 62

On Holy Saturday 70

During the Octave of Easter 76

4

Oh night that was my guide !
Oh darkness dearer than the morning's pride,
Oh night that joined the lover
To the belovèd bride
Transfiguring them each into the other.

Within my flowering breast
Which only for himself entire I save
He sank into his rest
And all my gifts I gave
Lulled by the airs with which the cedars wave.

Over the ramparts fanned
While the fresh wind was fluttering his tresses,
With his serenest hand
My neck he wounded, and
Suspended every sense with its caresses.

Lost to myself I stayed
My face upon my lover having laid
From all endeavour ceasing :
And all my cares releasing
Threw them amongst the lilies there to fade.

Saint John of the Cross, *Dark Night of the Soul*, verses 21–40, translated by Roy Campbell.

Proëm.

COMPLINE is the seventh and the laſt hour of divine service, and it is as much to say as a "fulfilling", for in the end thereof the seven hours of the divine service are fulfilled. And therewith also is ended and fulfilled speaking, eating, and drinking, and labouring, and all bodily business. So that after that time ought to be kept great ſtillness and ſtriĉt silence, not only from words, but also from all noise and deeds save only privy and soft prayer, holy thanksgiving, and bodily sleep.

For Compline betokeneth the end of man's life, or the end of the world, when the chosen of our Lord shall be delivered from all travail and woe and be brought to endless quiet and reſt. And therefore each person ought to dispose himself to bedward as if his bed were his grave. For as a man dieth or he be borne to his grave and buried, right so at Compline time ye should be disposed as if ye were in dying. And keep you so sober and ſtill afterward as if ye were dead from all bodily deeds and words. And in token thereof, in the response at Compline, ye pray our Lady to commend you in the hands and keeping of her Son, as a man dying sayeth *In manus tuas,* and commendeth his soul to God. And divers other things that ye say at Compline accordeth to the same.

From *The Myroure of oure Ladye* (15th century), edited by John Henry Blunt, London, 1873, pp. 164–195.

Ceremonial Notes.

WHEN Compline is said in quire, two, four, or six altar candles may be lit. The organ may be played where customary. Those in quire wear cassock and surplice and the clergy don the biretta when seated. There must be a Reader and one or two Cantors in addition to the Officiant. The Officiant may occupy the first place in the quire or the sedile.

The prayer Aperi, Dómine may be said, kneeling, before the Office. The Reader then goes to stand in the middle of quire, bows profoundly towards the Officiant—or, if the Officiant be not a deacon or priest, to the altar—and sings Jube, domne (or Dómine), benedícere. He remains bowed while the Officiant gives the blessing and then rises to say the short lesson facing the altar. At the words Tu autem Dómine miserére nobis, he genuflects towards the altar, then bows to both sides of the quire and returns to his place.

All make the sign of the Cross while the Officiant sings the ℣. Adjutórium nostrum. After singing the ℟. Qui fecit, Pater noster is said entirely in silence. All in quire then remain standing erect while the Officiant bows to say Confíteor. He strikes his breast thrice at the words mea culpa, mea culpa, mea máxima culpa and turns towards the quire as the words vobis fratres and vos fratres. He remains bowed while the quire say Misereátur and then stands erect while the quire bow to say Confíteor. They likewise strike the breast thrice at the mea culpa, &c., and turn towards the Officiant at the words tibi, pater and te pater. When the Officiant says Indulgéntiam they rise and make the sign of the Cross. If the Officiant be not a deacon or priest, all bow to say Confíteor and rise at Indulgéntiam.

While the Officiant sings the ℣. Convérte nos, all make the sign of the Cross over the heart with the thumb. At the ℣. Deus in adjutórium, they make the sign of the Cross as usual. The Cantor (both if there be two) sings the incipit of the antiphon Miserére and the first verse of the psalm Cum invocárem. At the end of the first half of the first verse, all in quire sit and the clergy cover themselves with the biretta. They remain seated until the antiphon Miserére is sung at the end of the four psalms, uncovering and bowing their heads at each Glória Patri. The Cantor or Cantors, however, rise each time they intone the first verse of each psalm.

At the end of the antiphon Miserére, all rise. At the first three lines of the last stanza of the hymn all bow towards the altar. The Officiant sings the Chapter. The Cantor or Cantors then go to the middle of the quire and sing the verses of the ℟. In manus tuas, to which the quire respond. All bow toward the altar at the Glória Patri. The Cantor or Cantors then sing the ℣. Custódi nos and return to their places. From there they sing the incipit of the antiphon Salva nos and the first verse of the canticle Nunc dimíttis. All make the sign of the Cross at the intonation of the canticle Nunc dimíttis, bow towards the altar at Glória Patri, and sit while the antiphon Salva nos is sung at the end.

If the Dominical *preces* follow, all stand, except on ferias of Advent and Lent, when all kneel. On said ferias, the quire remain kneeling while the Officiant stands to say the ℣. Dóminus vobíscum and the collect after the *preces*. Then all rise and the Cantor or Cantors sing the ℣. Benedicámus Dómino. The Officiant gives the final blessing and all make the sign of the Cross with him.

The anthem of the Blessed Virgin Mary is then said kneeling except on Saturdays and Sundays and during Eastertide. All remain kneeling while the Officiant rises to sing the ℣. and collect. Then all rise and the Officiant sings the ℣. Divínum auxílium. All remain standing while silently saying the concluding Pater noster, Ave María, and Credo. The prayer Sacrosánctæ may be said, kneeling, thereafter.

In many places, it is customary to perform the aspersion of holy water after Compline. The Officiant and a server carrying the holy water stoop and aspergill kneel at the centre of quire in front of the altar while the Cantor or Cantors intone the appropriate antiphon, according to the season. Meanwhile, the server gives the aspergill to the Officiant with the usual kisses and then the Officiant sprinkles everyone in quire, who remain kneeling throughout except on Saturdays, Sundays, and during Eastertide, when they stand.

Prayers before and after the Divine Office.

Before the Office is begun, it is commendable to say the following prayer, the singular number being used throughout, for which Pope Pius XI. granted an indulgence of three years (17 November 1933).

Aperi Dómine os meum ad benedicéndum nomen sanctum tuum : munda quoque cor meum ab ómnibus vanis, pervérsis et aliénis cogitatiónibus ; intelléctum illúmina, afféctum inflámma, ut digne, atténte ac devóte hoc Offícium recitáre váleam, et exaudíri mérear ante conspéctum divínæ Majestátis tuæ. Per Christum Dóminum nostrum. ℟. Amen.

Open thou my mouth, O Lord, to bless thy holy name : cleanse also my heart from all vain, perverse, and wandering thoughts ; enlighten my understanding, kindle my affections, that I may recite this Office with worthy attention and devotion, and may deserve to be heard in the presence of thy divine Majesty. Through Christ our Lord. ℟. Amen.

Dómine, in unióne illíus divínæ intentiónis, qua ipse in terris laudes Deo persolvísti, hanc tibi Horam persólvo.

O Lord, in union with that divine intention wherewith thou didst thyself praise God on earth, I offer to thee this Hour.

To those who devoutly say, kneeling, the following prayer after the Office, Pope Leo X. granted the remission of the defects and faults in its recital arising from human frailty, and Pope Pius XI. an indulgence of three years (1 December 1933).

Sacrosánctæ et indivíduæ Trinitáti, crucifíxi Dómini nostri

To the most holy and undivided Trinity, to the manhood of

Jesu Christi humanitáti, beatíssimæ et gloriosíssimæ sempérque Vírginis Maríæ fœcúndæ integritáti, et ómnium Sanctórum universitáti sit sempitérna laus, honor, virtus et glória ab omni creatúra, nobísque remíssio ómnium peccatórum, per infiníta sǽcula sæculórum. ℟. Amen.

℣. Beata víscera Maríæ Vírginis, quæ portavérunt ætérni Patris Fílium. ℟. Et beáta úbera, quæ lactavérunt Christum Dóminum.

our crucified Lord Jesus Christ, to the fruitful integrity of the most blessed and most glorious Virgin Mary, and to the host of all the saints be everlasting praise, honour, power, and glory, from every creature ; and to us the remission of all our sins, world without end. ℟. Amen.

℣. Blessed is the womb of the Virgin Mary, which bore the Son of the eternal Father. ℟. And blessed are the paps which gave suck to Christ the Lord.

Pater noster and Ave María are then said in silence.

Lord's Prayer, Angelic Salutation, & Symbol.

These three prayers are said in silence after the oration following the anthem of the Blessed Virgin Mary.

Pater noster, qui es in cælis : sanctificétur nomen tuum : advéniat regnum tuum : fiat volúntas tua, sicut in cælo, et in terra. Panem nostrum quotidiánum da nobis hódie : et dimítte nobis débita nostra, sicut et nos dimíttimus debitóribus nostris : et ne nos indúcas in tentatiónem : sed líbera nos a malo. Amen.

Our Father, who art in heaven, hallowed be thy name. Thy kingdom come. Thy will be done on earth as it is in heaven. Give us this day our daily bread. And forgive us our trespasses, as we forgive those who trespass against us. And lead us not into temptation, but deliver us from evil. Amen.

Ave María, grátia plena, Dóminus tecum : benedícta tu in muliéribus, et benedíctus fructus ventris tui Jesus. Sancta María, Mater Dei, ora pro nobis peccatóribus, nunc et in hora mortis nostræ. Amen.

Hail Mary, full of grace, the Lord is with thee : blessed art thou amongst women, and blessed is the fruit of thy womb, Jesus. Holy Mary, Mother of God, pray for us sinners, now and at the hour of our death. Amen.

Credo in Deum, Patrem omnipoténtem, creatórem cæli et terræ. Et in Jesum Christum, Fílium ejus únicum, Dóminum nostrum : qui concéptus est de Spíritu Sancto, natus ex María Vírgine : passus sub Póntio Piláto, cru-

I believe in God, the Father almighty, creator of heaven and earth. And in Jesus Christ, his only Son, our Lord : who was conceived by the Holy Ghost, born of the Virgin Mary, suffered under Pontius Pilate, was crucified,

cifíxus, mórtuus, et sepúltus : descéndit ad ínferos : tértia die resurréxit a mórtuis : ascéndit ad cælos, sedet ad déxteram Dei Patris omnipoténtis : inde ventúrus est judicáre vivos et mórtuos. Credo in Spíritum Sanctum, sanctam Ecclésiam cathólicam, Sanctórum communiónem, remissiónem peccatórum, carnis resurrectiónem, vitam ætérnam. Amen.

died and was buried : he descended into hell : the third day he arose again from the dead : he ascended into heaven, sitteth at the right hand of God the Father almighty : from thence he shall come to judge the living and the dead.   I believe in the Holy Ghost, the holy catholic Church, the communion of Saints, the forgiveness of sins, the resurrection of the body, life everlasting. Amen.

DIVINA PSALMODIA — EST CŒLESTIS — HYMNODIÆ — FILIA, QUÆ — CANITUR ASSIDUE — ANTE SEDEM — DEI ET AGNI. — Urbanus VIII.

✠

IN THE NAME OF THE HOLY AND UNDIVIDED TRINITY. AMEN.

HERE BEGINS THE HOUR OF COMPLINE ACCORDING TO THE ANCIENT ROMAN RITE.

The Reader asks for a blessing :

u-be dom-ne be-ne-dí-ce-re.
Grant, Father, a blessing.

❡ If the Officiant be not a deacon or priest, the Reader instead says Jube Dómine benedícere.

14

The Officiant gives the blessing :

N octem qui- é-tam et fi-nem perféctum concé-dat no-
May the almighty Lord grant us a quiet night and a perfect end.

bis Dómi-nus omní-po-tens. ℟. Amen.

The Reader says the short lesson :

1 Pet. 5. c

F ratres : Sóbri- i eśtó-te, et vi-gi-lá-te : qui- a adversá-
Brethren : Be sober and watch : because your adversary the devil, as

ri- us ve-śter di- á-bo-lus, tamquam le- o rú-gi- ens círcu- it,
a roaring lion, goeth about seeking whom he may devour.

quæ-rens quem dé-vo-ret : cu- i re-sí-śti- te fortes in fi- de.
Whom resist ye strong in faith.

Tu au-tem Dómi-ne mi-se-ré-re no-bis. ℟. De- o grá- ti- as.
But thou, O Lord, have mercy on us.   *Thanks be to God.*

The Officiant then sings :

℣.

A d-ju-tó-ri- um nóstrum in nómi-ne Dómi-ni.

Our help is in the name of the Lord.

℟. Qui fe-cit cæ-lum et terram.

Who made heaven and earth.

Pater noster is said in silence. Then the Officiant says entirely *recto tono* in a low voice :

Confíteor Deo omnipoténti, beátæ Maríæ semper Vírgini, beáto Michaéli Archángelo, beáto Joánni Baptístæ, sanctis Apóstolis Petro et Paulo, ómnibus Sanctis, et vobis fratres : quia peccávi nimis cogitatióne, verbo et ópere : mea culpa, mea culpa, mea máxima culpa. Ideo precor beátam Maríam semper Vírginem, beátum Michaélem Archángelum, beátum Joánnem Baptístam, sanctos Apóstolos Petrum et Paulum, omnes Sanctos, et vos fratres, oráre pro me ad Dóminum Deum nostrum.

I confess to almighty God, to blessed Mary ever Virgin, to blessed Michael the Archangel, to blessed John the Baptist, to the holy Apostles Peter and Paul, to all the Saints, and you, my brethren, that I have sinned exceedingly in thought, word, and deed : through my fault, through my fault, through my most grievous fault. Therefore I beseech blessed Mary ever Virgin, blessed Michael the Archangel, blessed John the Baptist, the holy Apostles Peter and Paul, all the Saints, and you, my brethren, to pray for me to the Lord our God.

16

Misereátur tui omnípotens Deus, et dimíssis peccátis tuis, perdúcat te ad vitam ætérnam. ℞. Amen.

May almighty God be merciful to thee, and forgiving thy sins, bring thee to everlasting life. ℞. Amen.

Confíteor Deo omnipoténti, beátæ Maríæ semper Vírgini, beáto Michaéli Archángelo, beáto Joánni Baptístæ, sanctis Apóstolis Petro et Paulo, ómnibus Sanctis, et tibi pater : quia peccávi nimis cogitatióne, verbo et ópere : mea culpa, mea culpa, mea máxima culpa. Ideo precor beátam Maríam semper Vírginem, beátum Michaélem Archángelum, beátum Joánnem Baptístam, sanctos Apóstolos Petrum et Paulum, omnes Sanctos, et te pater, oráre pro me ad Dóminum, Deum nostrum.

I confess to almighty God, to blessed Mary ever Virgin, blessed Michael the Archangel, blessed John the Baptist, the holy Apostles Peter and Paul, to all the Saints, and to you, Father, that I have sinned exceedingly in thought, word, and deed : through my fault, through my fault, through my most grievous fault. Therefore I beseech blessed Mary ever Virgin, blessed Michael the Archangel, blessed John the Baptist, the holy Apostles Peter and Paul, all the Saints, and you, Father, to pray to the Lord our God for me.

The Officiant continues :

Misereátur vestri omnípotens Deus, et dimíssis peccátis vestris, perdúcat vos ad vitam ætérnam. ℞. Amen.

May almighty God be merciful to you, and forgiving your sins, bring you to everlasting life. ℞. Amen.

Indulgéntiam, absolutiónem et remissiónem peccatórum nostrórum tríbuat nobis omnípotens et miséricors Dóminus. ℟. Amen.

May the almighty and merciful Lord grant us pardon, absolution, and remission of our sins. ℟. Amen.

❡ If the Officiant be not a deacon or priest, after Pater noster all say :

Confíteor Deo omnipoténti, beátæ Maríæ semper Vírgini, beáto Michaéli Archángelo, beáto Joánni Baptístæ, sanctis Apóstolis Petro et Paulo, et ómnibus Sanctis : quia peccávi nimis cogitatióne, verbo et ópere : mea culpa, mea culpa, mea máxima culpa. Ideo precor beátam Maríam semper Vírginem, beátum Michaélem Archángelum, beátum Joánnem Baptístam, sanctos Apóstolos Petrum et Paulum, et omnes Sanctos, oráre pro me ad Dóminum, Deum nostrum.

I confess to almighty God, to blessed Mary ever Virgin, blessed Michael the Archangel, blessed John the Baptist, the holy Apostles Peter and Paul, and to all the Saints, that I have sinned exceedingly in thought, word, and deed : through my fault, through my fault, through my most grievous fault. Therefore I beseech blessed Mary ever Virgin, blessed Michael the Archangel, blessed John the Baptist, the holy Apostles Peter and Paul, and all the Saints to pray to the Lord our God for me.

Misereátur nostri omnípotens Deus, et dimíssis peccátis nostris, perdúcat nos ad vitam ætérnam. ℟. Amen.

May almighty God have mercy on us, forgive us our sins, and bring us to everlasting life. ℟. Amen.

Indulgéntiam, absolutiónem et remissiónem peccatórum nostrórum tríbuat nobis omnípotens et miséricors Dóminus. ℟. Amen.

May the almighty and merciful Lord grant us pardon, absolution, and remission of our sins. ℟. Amen.

18

The Officiant then sings :

℣.

Convérte nos De- us sa-lu-tá-ris noster. ℟. Et a-vérte
Turn us then, O God, our saviour. *And let*

i- ram tu- am a no-bis. ℣. De- us in adju-tó-ri- um me-
thy anger cease from us. *O God, come to my assistance.*

um intende. ℟. Dómi-ne ad adju-vándum me fe-stí-na.
O Lord, make haste to help me.

Gló-ri- a Pa-tri, et Fí- li- o, et Spí-ri-tu- i Sancto. Si-cut e-rat
Glory be to the Father, and to the Son, and to the Holy Ghost. As it was in the

in princí-pi- o et nunc, et semper, et in sǽ-cu-la sæ-cu-ló-
beginning, is now, and ever shall be, world without end.

rum. Amen. Alle-lu-ia.

❡ From the Saturday before Septuagesima to Spy Wednesday, the following is
said instead of Allelúia :

Laus ti-bi Dómi-ne Rex æ-ternæ gló-ri- æ.
Praise be to thee, O Lord, King of eternal glory.

¶ During the year.

Ant.
8. G

M i-se-ré- re.

¶ In Eastertide.

Ant.
8. G

A l- le-lú- ia.

The Cantor begins the psalm, and the quire joins him after the mediant.

Psalm 4.

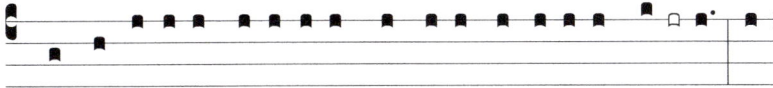

1. *Cum in*vo-cá-rem exaudí-vit me De- us jus-tí- ti- æ me- æ : * in
When I invocated, the God of my justice heard me : in

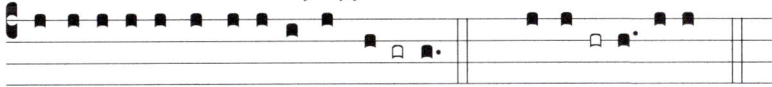

tri-bu-la-ti- ó-ne di- la-*tás-ti* mi- hi. Flex : pecc*á*-re : †
tribulation thou hast enlarged to me.

2. Miserére mei, * et exáudi ora-tió*nem* meam.

2. Have mercy on me, and hear my prayer.

3. Fílii hóminum úsquequo gravi corde ? * ut quid dilígitis vanitátem et quǽri*tis men*dácium ?

3. Ye sons of men, how long are you of heavy heart ? Why love you vanity and seek lying ?

4. Et scitóte quóniam mirificávit Dóminus sanctum suum : * Dóminus exáudiet me cum clamávero ad eum.

4. And know ye that that our Lord hath made his holy one marvellous : our Lord will hear me when I shall cry to him.

5. Irascímini, et nolíte peccáre : † quæ dícitis in córdibus vestris, * in cubílibus vestris compungímini.

5. Be ye angry, and sin not : the things you say in your hearts, in your chambers be ye sorry for.

6. Sacrificáte sacrifícium justítiæ, † et speráte in Dómino. * Multi dicunt : quis osténdit nobis bona ?

6. Sacrifice ye the sacrifice of justice, and hope in our Lord. Many say : Who sheweth us good things ?

7. Signátum est super nos lumen vultus tui Dómine : * dedísti lætítiam in corde meo.

7. The light of thy countenance, O Lord, is signed upon us : thou hast given gladness in my heart.

8. A fructu fruménti, vini et ólei sui * multiplicáti sunt.

8. By the fruit of their corn, and wine, and oil they are multiplied.

9. In pace in idípsum * dórmiam et requiéscam.

9. In peace in the selfsame I will sleep and rest.

10. Quóniam tu Dómine singuláriter in spe * constituísti me.

10. Because thou, Lord, hast singularly settled me in hope.

11. Glória Patri, et Fílio, * et Spirítui Sancto.

11. Glory be to the Father, and to the Son, and to the Holy Ghost.

12. Sicut erat in princípio, et nunc, et semper, * et in sæcula sæculórum. Amen.

12. As it was in the beginning is now, and ever shall be, world without end. Amen.

25

Psalm 30.

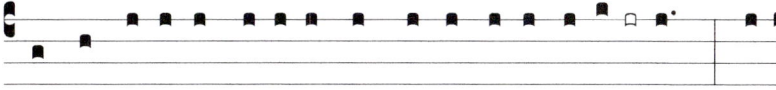

1. *In te* Dómi-ne spe-rá-vi, non confúndar in æ-tér- num : * in
In thee, O Lord, have I hoped, let me not be confounded forever :   *in*

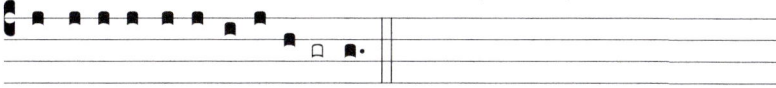

jus-tí- ti- a tu- a *lí-be-ra* me.
thy justice deliver me.

2. Inclína ad me aurem tuam, *
accélera ut *éruas* me.

2. Incline thine ear to me, make haste to deliver me.

3. Esto mihi in Deum protectó-rem, et in domum refúgii, * ut sal-*vum me fácias.*

3. Be unto me for a God protec-tor, and for a house of refuge, that thou mayest save me.

4. Quóniam fortitúdo mea et re-fúgium meum es tu : * et prop-ter nomen tuum dedúces me, et *enútries* me.

4. Because thou art my strength and my refuge : and for thy name thou wilt conduct me, and wilt nourish me.

5. Edúces me de láqueo hoc, quem abscondérunt mihi : * quó-niam tu es protéctor meus.

5. Thou wilt bring me out of this snare, which they have hid for me : because thou art my protector.

6. In manus tuas comméndo spí-ritum meum : * redemísti me Dó-mine Deus *veritátis.*

6. Into thy hands I commend my spirit : thou hast redeemed me, O Lord God of truth.

7. Glória Patri, et F̲ílio, * et Spirí-
tui San̲cto.

7. Glory be to the Father, and to
the Son, and to the Holy Ghoſt.

8. Sicut erat in princípio, et
nunc, et s̲emper, * et in sǽcula sæcu*lórum*. A̲men.

8. As it was in the beginning is
now, and ever shall be, world without end. Amen.

Psalm 90.

1. *Qui há*-bi- tat in adju-tó-ri- o Altís̲-simi, * in pro-tec-ti- ó-ne
He that dwelleth in the help of the Highest, shall abide in the protection of the

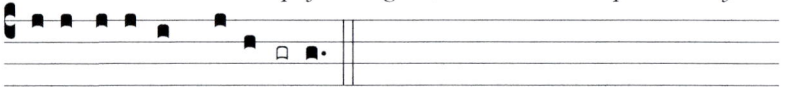

De- i cæ-li *commo-*rá̲-bi-tur.
God of heaven.

2. Dicet Dómino : Suscéptor
meus es tu, et refúgium m̲eum : *
Deus meus sper*ábo in* e̲um.

2. He shall say to our Lord :
Thou art my protector, and my
refuge : my God, I will hope in
him.

3. Quóniam ipse liberávit me de
láqueo ven̲ántium, * et a *verbo*
á̲spero.

3. Because he hath delivered me
from the snare of the hunters, and
from the sharp word.

4. Scápulis suis obumbrábit
t̲ibi : * et sub pennis *ejus ſpe*r̲ábis.

4. With his shoulders shall he
will overshadow thee : and under
his wings thou shalt hope.

5. Scuto circúmdabit te véritas ejus : * non timébis a timóre noctúrno.

6. A sagítta volánte in die, † a negótio perambulánte in ténebris : * ab incúrsu, et dæmónio meridiáno.

7. Cadent a látere tuo mille, † et decem míllia a dextris tuis : * ad te autem non appropinquábit.

8. Verúmtamen óculis tuis considerábis : * et retributiónem peccatórum vidébis.

9. Quóniam tu es Dómine spes mea : * Altíssimum posuísti refúgium tuum.

10. Non accédet ad te malum : * et flagéllum non appropinquábit tabernáculo tuo.

11. Quóniam Angelis suis mandávit de te : * ut custódiant te in ómnibus viis tuis.

12. In mánibus portábunt te : * ne forte offéndas ad lápidem pedem tuum.

5. With shield shall his truth compass thee : thou shalt not be afraid of the fear in the night.

6. Of the arrow flying in the day, of business walking in darkness : of invasion, and the midday devil.

7. A thousand shall fall on thy side, and ten thousand on thy right hand : but to thee it shall not approach.

8. But thou shalt consider with thine eyes : and shalt see the retribution of sinners.

9. Because thou, O Lord, art my hope : thou hast made the Highest thy refuge.

10. There shall no evil come to thee : and the scourge shall not approach to thy tabernacle.

11. Because he hath given his angels charge of thee ; that they keep thee in all thy ways.

12. In their hands they shall bear thee : lest perhaps thou knock thy foot against a stone.

13. Super áspidem et basilíscum ambulábis : * et conculcábis leónem *et dracó*nem.

13. Upon the asp and the basilisk thou shalt walk : and thou shalt tread upon the lion and the dragon.

14. Quóniam in me sperávit, liberábo eum : * prótegam eum quóniam cognóvit *nomen* meum.

14. Because he hath hoped in me, I will deliver him : I will protect him because he hath known my name.

15. Clamábit ad me, et ego exáudiam eum : † cum ipso sum in tribulatióne : * erípiam eum, et glorifi*cábo* eum.

15. He shall cry to me, and I will hear him : with him I am in tribulation : I will deliver him, and will glorify him.

16. Longitúdine diérum replébo eum : * et osténdam illi salu*táre* meum.

16. With length of days I will replenish him : and I will shew him my salvation.

17. Glória Patri, et Fílio, * et Spi-rí*tui* Sancto.

17. Glory be to the Father, and to the Son, and to the Holy Ghost.

18. Sicut erat in princípio, et nunc, et semper, * et in sǽcula sæcu*lórum*. Amen.

18. As it was in the beginning is now, and ever shall be, world without end. Amen.

Psalm 133.

1. *Ecce* nunc be-ne-dí-ci-te Dómi-num, * omnes *servi* Dómi-ni :
   Lo ! now bless our Lord, all ye the servants of our Lord :

2. Qui ſtatis in domo Dómini, * in átriis domus *Dei* nostri.

2. Which ſtand in the house of our Lord, in the courts of the house of our God.

3. In nóctibus extóllite manus veſtras in sancta, * et bened*ícite* Dóminum.

3. In the nights lift up your hands unto the holy places, and bless ye our Lord.

4. Benedícat te Dóminus ex Sion, * qui fecit cæ*lum et* terram.

4. Our Lord of Sion bless thee, who made heaven and earth.

5. Glória Patri, et Fílio, * et Spirí-*tui* Sancto.

5. Glory be to the Father, and to the Son, and to the Holy Ghoſt.

6. Sicut erat in princípio, et nunc, et semper, * et in sǽcula sæ-cul*órum*. Amen.

6. As it was in the beginning is now, and ever shall be, world without end. Amen.

℣ During the year.

Ant.

M i-se-ré- re mi-hi Dómi-ne, et exáudi o- ra- ti- ó-nem
Have mercy on me, O Lord, and hearken to my prayer.

me- am.

℣ In Eaſtertide.

Ant.

A l- le-lú- ia, al-le-lú-ia, al-le-lú- ia.

Hymn.

The melody of the hymn Te lucis ante términum varies according to the season and feasts, as indicated on page 50. The settings for Sundays and ferias *per annum* and for feasts without a proper tone are as follows :

On ferias and simples.

8.

T e lu-cis ante térmi-num, Re-rum Cre- á-tor, póscimus,
Before the closing of the light, we beseech thee, Creator of all things,

Ut só-li-ta cleménti- a, Sis præ-sul ad custó-di- am. 2. Pro-cul
that in thy wonted clemency, thou be our guardsman for the watch. Far off

re-cé-dant sómni- a, Et nócti- um phantásma-ta : Hostémque
let dreams and phantoms of the night depart. Restrain our foe lest our bodies

nostrum cómprime, Ne pol-lu- ántur córpo-ra. 3. Præsta, Pa-ter
be defiled.   *Grant this, O*

omní-po-tens, Per Je-sum Chri-stum Dómi-num, Qui te-cum in
Father Almighty, through Jesus Christ the Lord, who reigns forever with thee

perpé-tu- um, Regnat cum Sancto Spí- ri-tu.   A- men.
together with the Holy Ghost.

❡ On ordinary Saturdays, Sundays, semidoubles, & major and minor doubles.

8.

Te lu-cis ante térmi-num, Re-rum Cre- á-tor, póscimus,

Ut só-li-ta cleménti- a,   Sis præ-sul ad custó-di- am. 2. Pro-cul

re-cé-dant sómni- a,   Et nócti- um phantásma-ta : Hostémque

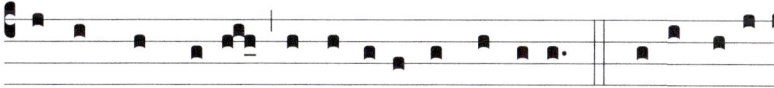

nostrum cómprime,   Ne pol-lu- ántur córpo-ra. 3. Præsta, Pa-ter

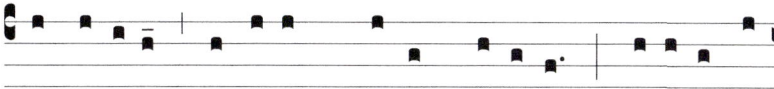

omní-po-tens, Per Je-sum Chri-stum Dómi-num, Qui te-cum in

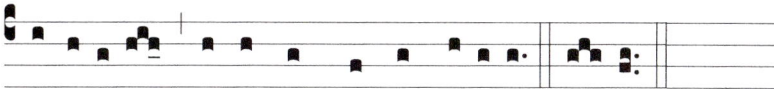

perpé-tu- um, Regnat cum Sancto Spí- ri-tu.   A- men.

¶ On doubles of the first and second class.

4.

Te lu-cis an-te térmi- num, Re-rum Cre- á- tor, pó-sci-

mus, Ut só-li- ta clemén-ti- a, Sis præ-sul ad custó-di- am.

2. Pro-cul re- cé-dant sómni- a, Et nócti- um phantásma- ta :

Hostémque nostrum cómpri-me, Ne pol-lu- án-tur córpo- ra.

3. Præsta, Pa- ter omní-po- tens, Per Je-sum Chri-stum Dó-mi-

num, Qui te-cum in perpé- tu- um, Regnat cum Sancto Spí-

ri- tu. A- men.

Chapter.

Jer. 14. b

Tu au-tem in no-bis es, Dómi-ne, † et nomen sanctum
But thou, O Lord, art in us, and thy holy name is invocated upon

tu- um invo-cá-tum est su-per nos : * ne de-re-línquas nos, Dó-
us : forsake us not, O Lord our God.

mi-ne, De- us noster. ℟. De- o grá-ti- as.
Thanks be to God.

Short Responsory.

¶ During the year.

℟. In ma-nus tu- as Dó-mi-ne, * Commendo spí- ri- tum me-
Into thy hands, O Lord,   I commend my spirit.

um. Repeat : In ma-nus. ℣. Red-e-mí-sti nos Dómi-ne   De- us
Thou hast redeemed us, O Lord God of truth.

ve- ri- tá- tis. * Comméndo. ℣. Gló-ri- a Pa-tri,   et Fí- li- o,
Glory be to the Father, and to the Son,

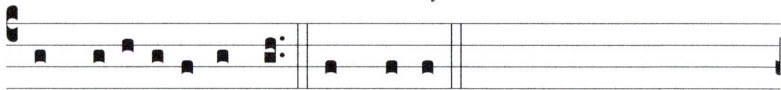

et Spi- rí-tu- i Sanĉto.   In ma-nus.
and to the Holy Ghost.

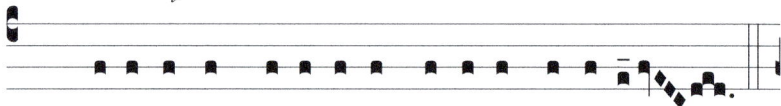

℣. Cuŝtó-di nos Dómi-ne ut pu-píl-lam ó-cu- li.
Keep us, Lord, as the apple of the eye.

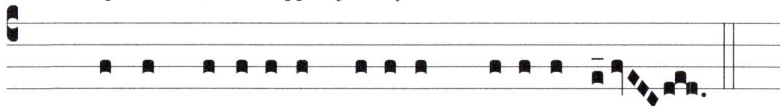

℟. Sub umbra a-lá-rum tu- á-rum pró-te-ge nos.
Under the shadow of thy wings protect us.

❡ During Passiontide, the ℣. Glória Patri is not said, but the ℟. In manus is repeated inŝtead. On feaŝts, however, the ℣. Glória Patri is said as usual.

❡ During Advent.

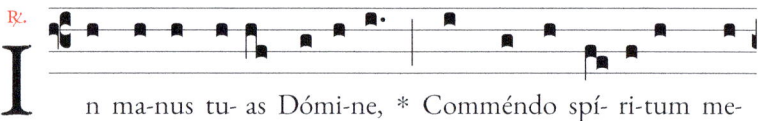

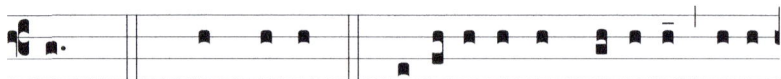

℟. I n ma-nus tu- as Dómi-ne, * Comméndo spí- ri-tum me-

um. Repeat: In ma-nus. ℣. Re-demí-ŝti nos Dómi-ne, De- us

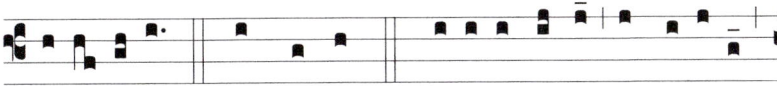

ve- ri- tá- tis. * Comméndo. ℣. Gló-ri- a Pa-tri, et Fí- li- o,

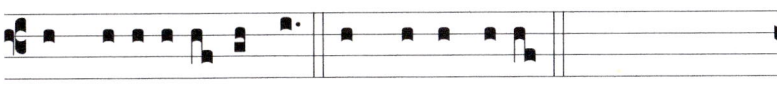

et Spi- rí-tu- i Sancto. In ma-nus tu- as.

℣. Custó-di nos Dómi-ne ut pu-píl-lam ó-cu-li.

℟. Sub umbra a-lárum tu- árum pró- tege nos.

¶ In Eastertide.

℟.

In ma-nus tu- as Dómi- ne, comméndo spí- ri- tum me-

um. * Al-le- lú- ia, al-le-lú- ia. Repeat: In ma-nus. ℣. Re-de-

mí-sti nos Dómi-ne, De- us ve-ri-tá- tis. * Al-le- lú- ia, al-le-lú-

ia. ℣. Gló-ri- a Pa-tri, et Fí- li- o, et Spi- rí-tu- i Sancto.

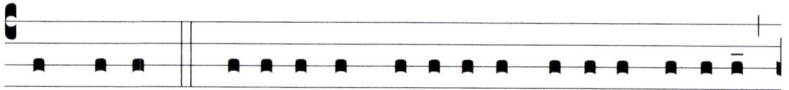

In ma-nus. ℣. Custó-di nos Dómi-ne ut pu-píl-lam ó-cu-li,

℞. Sub umbra a-lárum tu-árum pró-te-ge nos,

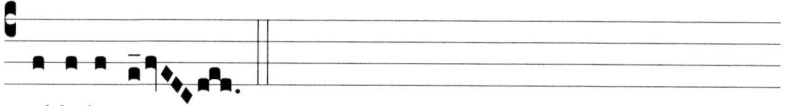

al-le-lú-ia.

Ant.
3. a
S alva nos.

Canticle of Simeon (Luke 2. e).

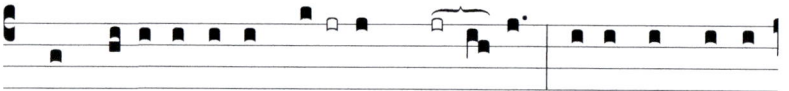

1. *Nunc di*mít-tis servum tu- um, Dó-mi-ne, * se-cúndum verbum
Now thou dost dismiss thy servant, O Lord, according to thy word in peace :

tu-um in pa- ce : 2. *Qui-a* vi-dé-runt *&c.* 3. Quod pa-rá-sti *

2. *Quia* vidérunt óculi mei * salutáre tuum :

2. Because my eyes have seen thy
salvation :

3. Quod parásti * ante fáciem ómnium populórum :

3. Which thou hast prepared before the face of all peoples :

4. *Lumen* ad revelatiónem Géntium, * et glóriam plebis tuæ Israel.

4. A light to the revelation of the Gentiles, and the glory of thy people Israel.

5. *Glóri*a Patri, et Fílio, * et Spirítui Sancto.

5. Glory be to the Father, and to the Son, and to the Holy Ghost.

6. *Sicut* erat in princípio, et nunc, et semper, * et in sǽcula sæculórum. Amen.

6. As it was in the beginning is now, and ever shall be, world without end. Amen.

Ant.

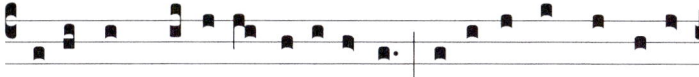

S alva nos, Dómi- ne, vi- gi- lántes, custó-di nos dormi- én-
Protect us, Lord, while we are awake and safeguard us while we sleep,

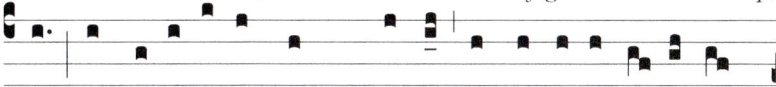

tes : ut vi- gi- lémus cum Chri- sto, et requi- e- scámus in
that we may keep watch with Christ, and rest in peace.

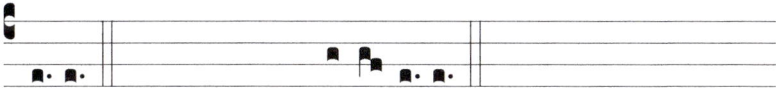

pa- ce. In Eastertide is added : Al-le- lú- ia.

34

Dominical Preces.

¶ The following Dominical *preces* are always said except on days of double rite and within octaves. On ferias of Advent and Lent they are said kneeling.

Ký-ri- e e-lé- i-son. ℟. Chri-ste e-lé- i-son. Ký-ri- e
Lord, have mercy. Christ, have mercy. Lord have mercy.

e-lé- i-son.

Pa-ter noster. continued silently until ℣. Et ne nos indú-cas
Padre nuestro. *And lead us not into*

in tenta-ti- ó-nem. ℟. Sed lí-be-ra nos a ma-lo.
temptation. *But deliver us from evil.*

Cre-do in De- um. continued silently until ℣. Carnis re-sur-
I believe. *The resurrection*

rec-ti- ó- nem ℟. Vi-tam æ-térnam. A- men.
of the body. *Life everlasting.*

℣. Benedíctus es Dómine Deus patrum nostrórum. ℟. Et laudábilis et gloriósus in sǽcula.

℣. Benedicámus Patrem et Fílium cum Sancto Spíritu. ℟. Laudémus, et superexaltémus eum in sǽcula.

℣. Benedíctus es Dómine in firmaménto cæli. ℟. Et laudábilis, et gloriósus, et superexaltátus in sǽcula.

℣. Benedícat et custódiat nos omnípotens et miséricors Dóminus. ℟. Amen.

℣. Dignáre Dómine nocte ista. ℟. Sine peccáto nos custodíre.

℣. Miserére nostri Dómine. ℟. Miserére nostri.

℣. Fiat misericórdia tua Dómine super nos. ℟. Quemádmodum sperávimus in te.

℣. Dómine exáudi oratiónem meam. ℟. Et clamor meus ad te véniat.

℣. Dominus vobíscum. ℟. Et cum spíritu tuo.

℣. Blessed art thou, O Lord the God of our fathers. ℟. And laudable and glorious forever.

℣. Let us bless the Father and the Son with the Holy Ghost. ℟. Let us praise and exalt him above all forever.

℣. Blessed art thou in the firmament of heaven. ℟. And laudable, and glorious, and exalted above all forever.

℣. May the almighty and merciful Lord bless and keep us. ℟. Amen.

℣. Vouchsafe, O Lord, this night. ℟. To keep us without sin.

℣. Have mercy upon us, O Lord. ℟. Have mercy upon us.

℣. Let thy mercy, O Lord, be made upon us. ℟. As we have hoped in thee.

℣. Lord, hear my prayer. ℟. And let my cry come unto thee.

℣. The Lord be with you. ℟. And with thy spirit.

❡ The last ℣. is said even when the Dominical *preces* are omitted. But if the Officiant be not a priest, he only says the ℣. Dómine exáudi oratiónem meam.

Then the Officiant says the following collect :

O - rémus. Ví- si- ta, quǽ-sumus Dómi-ne, ha-bi-ta-ti- ó-
Let us pray. Visit, we beseech thee, O Lord, this habitation, and

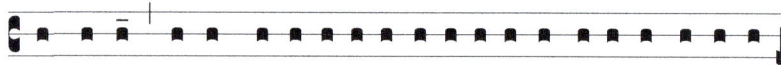

nem i-stam, et omnes insí-di- as i-nimí-ci ab e- a lónge re-pél-
drive far from it all the snares of the enemy :

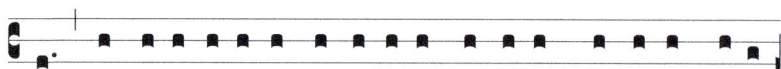

le : † Ange- li tu- i sancti há-bi- tent in e- a, qui nos in pa-*ce*
let thine holy angels dwell herein to keep us in peace,

custó-di- ant ; * et be-ne-dí-cti- o tu- a sit su-per nos semper.
and may thy blessing be always upon us.

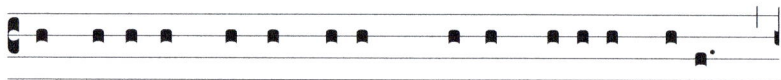

Per Dómi-num nostrum Je-sum Chri-stum Fí- li- um tu- um : †
Through Jesus Christ, thy Son our Lord, who liveth and reigneth with thee,

qui te-cum vi-vit et regnat in u-ni-tá-te Spí- ri-tus Sancti De- us, *
in the unity of the Holy Ghost, God, world without end.

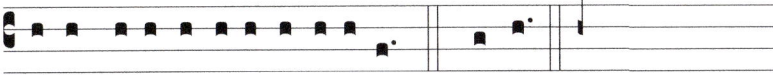

per ómni- a sǽ-cu-la sæ-cu-<u>ló</u>-rum. ℟. Amen.

℣. Dominus vo<u>bí</u>scum. ℟. Et cum spíritu <u>tuo</u>.

℣. The Lord be with you. ℟. And with thy spirit.

❡ If the Officiant be not a deacon or priest, he says instead :

℣. Dómine exáudi oratiónem <u>me</u>am. ℟. Et clamor meus ad te <u>vé</u>niat.

℣. Lord, hear my prayer. ℟. And let my cry come unto thee.

℣.

B e-ne-di-cámus Dómi-no. ℟. De- o grá- ti- as.
Let us bless the Lord. *Thanks be to God.*

The Officiant, even if he be not deacon, says the blessing *recto tono* in a low voice :

Benedícat et custódiat nos omnípotens et miséricors Dóminus, Pater, et Fílius, et Spíritus Sanctus. ℟. Amen.

May the almighty and merciful Lord, the Father, the Son, and the Holy Ghost, bless and keep us. ℟. Amen.

Then one of the anthems of Our Lady on the following page is sung according to the season. After the collect of the antiphon the Officiant sings *recto tono* in a low voice :

℣. Divínum auxílium máneat semper nobíscum. ℟. Amen.

℣. May the divine assistance remain with us always. ℟. Amen.

Pater noster, Ave María, and Credo are then said in silence.

✛

Anthems of the Blessed Virgin Mary.

The anthem is sung kneeling except on Saturday and Sunday and during Eastertide.

¶ From the Saturday before the first Sunday of Advent until second Compline of Candlemas inclusive.

Simple 5.

A l- ma * Re-demptó- ris Ma- ter, quæ pérvi- a cæ-li
Kindly Mother of the Redeemer, who art ever of heaven the open

porta ma-nes, Et stel-la ma-ris, succúrre ca-dénti súrge-re qui
gate, and the star of the sea, succour a falling people, which fain would rise;

cu-rat pópu-lo : Tu quæ ge-nu- í-sti, na-tú-ra mi-ránte, tu- um
thou who didst give birth, while nature marvelled how, to thy holy Creator:

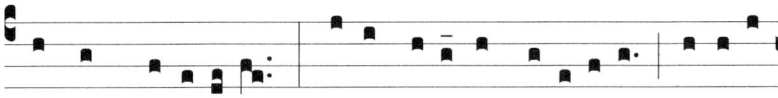

sanctum Ge-ni-tó-rem : Virgo pri- us ac posté-ri- us, Gabri- é-

Virgin both before and after, from Gabriel's mouth, accepting that Hail,

lis ab o-re sumens il-lud A-ve, pecca-tó-rum mi- se- ré- re.

have mercy on sinners.

Solemn
5.

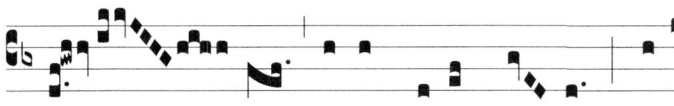

A l- ma * Re-demptó-ris Ma- ter, quæ

pér-vi- a cæ-li por-ta ma- nes, Et stel- la ma- ris, suc-

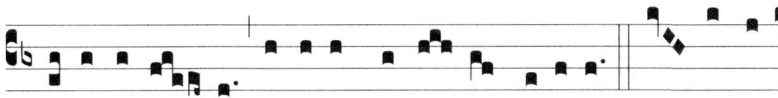

cúrre ca-dén- ti súrge-re qui cu- rat pópu-lo : Tu quæ ge-

nu- í- sti, na-tú- ra mi-rán- te, tu- um sanctum Ge- ni-tó-

rem : Vir- go pri- us ac po-sté- ri- us, Gabri- é- lis ab

40

o- re sumens il-lud A-ve, * pecca-tó-rum mi-se-ré- re.

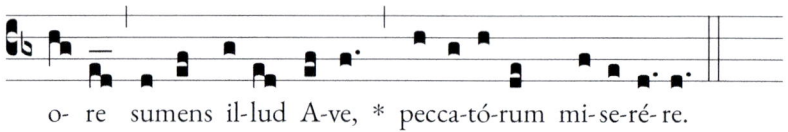

¶ During Advent :

℣. Angelus Dómini nuntiávit Maríæ. ℟. Et concépit de Spíritu Sancto.

Orémus.

Grátiam tuam, quǽsumus Dómine, méntibus nostris infúnde : † ut, qui, Ángelo nuntiánte, Christi Fílii tui incarnatió*nem cog*nóvimus ; * per passiónem ejus et crucem ad resurrectiónis glóriam perducámur. Per eúndem Christum Dóminum nóstrum. ℟. Amen.

℣. The Angel of the Lord announced unto Mary. ℟. And she conceived of the Holy Ghost.

Let us pray.

Pour forth, we beseech thee, O Lord, thy grace into our hearts : that as we have known the incarnation of thy Son Jesus Christ by the message of an Angel, so by his passion and cross we may be brought unto the glory of his resurrection. Through the same Christ our Lord. ℟. Amen.

¶ From first Compline of Christmas until second Compline of Candlemas :

℣. Post partum Virgo invioláta permansísti. ℟. Dei Génitrix, intercéde pro nobis.

Orémus.

Deus, qui salútis ætérnæ, beátæ Maríæ virginitáte fecúnda, humáno géneri prǽmia præstitísti : † tríbue, quǽsumus ; ut ipsam pro nobis intercédere *sen-*

℣. After childbirth, O Virgin, thou didst remain undefiled. ℟. Intercede for us, O Mother of God.

Let us pray.

O God, who, by the fruitful virginity of blessed Mary, hast bestowed upon mankind the rewards of eternal salvation : grant, we beseech thee, that we may feel

*ti*ámus, * per quam merúimus auc-
tórem vitæ suscípere, Dóminum
nóstrum Jesum Christum Fílium
tuum. ℞. Amen.

her intercession for us, through
whom we have been found worthy to receive the author of life,
Our Lord Jesus Christ thy Son.
℞. Amen.

❡ From Compline of 2 February (even if Candlemas be transferred) until Compline of Spy Wednesday inclusive.

Simple 6.

A - ve Re-gí-na cæ-ló-rum, * A-ve Dómi-na Ange-ló-
Hail, O Queen of heaven ! hail, O Lady of Angels !

rum : Salve ra-dix, salve porta, Ex qua mundo lux est orta :
Hail thou root, hail thou gate, from whom unto the world a light has

Gaude Virgo glo-ri- ó-sa, Su-per omnes spe-ci- ó-sa : Va- le, o
arisen. Rejoice, O glorious Virgin, lovely beyond all others. Farewell,

valde de-có- ra, Et pro no- bis Chri-stum ex-ó- ra.
O most beautiful maiden, and pray for us to Christ.

Solemn 6.

A - ve * Re-gí-na cæ- ló- rum, A- ve Dómi-na Ange-ló- rum : Sal- ve ra-dix, salve porta, Ex qua

mun- do lux est or- ta : Gaude Vir-go glo-ri- ó- sa, Su-per

o- mnes spe-ci- ó- sa : Va- le, o val-de de-có- ra,

Et pro no- bis Chri- stum * ex-ó- ra.

℣. Dignáre me laudáre te Virgo sacráta. ℟. Da mihi virtútem contra hostes tuos.

Orémus.

Concéde, miséricors Deus, fragilitáti nostræ præsídium ; † ut, qui sanctæ Dei Genetrícis memóriam ágimus, * intercessiónis eius auxílio, a nostris iniquitátibus resurgámus. Per eúndem Christum Dóminum nóstrum. ℟. Amen.

℣. Vouchsafe that I may praise thee, O holy Virgin. ℟. Give me strength against thine enemies.

Let us pray.

Grant, O merciful God, to our weakness thy protection, that we who commemorate the holy Mother of God may, by the help of her intercession, arise from our iniquities. Through the same Christ our Lord. ℟. Amen.

¶ From first Compline of Easter Sunday until Compline of Friday after Pentecost.

Simple
6.

Re-gí-na cæ-li * læ-tá-re, al-le-lú-ia : Qui- a quem me-
O Queen of heaven rejoice ! alleluia,   For he whom thou

ru- í-sti portá-re, al-le-lú-ia : Re-surréx-it, si-cut dix-it, al-le- lú-
didst merit to bear, alleluia,   Hath arisen as he said, alleluia,

ia : O-ra pro no-bis De- um, al-le-lú- ia.
Pray for us to God, alleluia.

Solemn
6.

Re-gí-na cæ-li * læ- tá-   re, al-le- lú-

ia : Qui- a quem me- ru- í-sti por-

tá- re, al-le-   lú-ia : Re-sur-réx-   it, si-cut dix-it,

44

al-le- lú-ia : O- ra pro no-bis De- um, al-le-

* ** lú- ia.

℣. Gaude et lætáre Virgo María, allelúia. ℟. Quia surréxit Dóminus vere, allelúia.

Orémus.

Deus, qui per resurrectiónem Fílii tui, Dómini nostri Jesu Christi, mundum lætificáre dignátus es : † præsta, quǽsumus ; ut, per eíus Genetrícem Vírginem Maríam, * perpétuæ capiámus gáudia vitæ. Per eúndem Christum Dóminum nóstrum. ℟. Amen.

℣. Rejoice and be glad, O Virgin Mary, alleluia. ℟. Because the Lord is truly risen, alleluia.

Let us pray.

O God, who through the resurrection of thy Son, our Lord Jesus Christ, didst vouchsafe to gladden the world : grant, we beseech thee, that through his Mother, the Virgin Mary, we may obtain the joys of everlasting life. Through the same Christ our Lord. ℟. Amen.

❡ From first Compline of Trinity Sunday until Compline of Saturday before the first Sunday of Advent exclusive.

Simple 5.

Salve, Re-gí-na, * ma-ter mi-se-ri-córdi- æ : Vi- ta, dul-
Hail, O Queen, Mother of Mercy, our life, our sweetness, and our

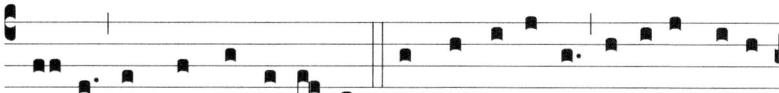

cé- do, et spes noſtra, sal-ve. Ad te clamámus, éxsu-les, fí- li-
hope, hail ! *To thee do we exiles cry out, the sons*

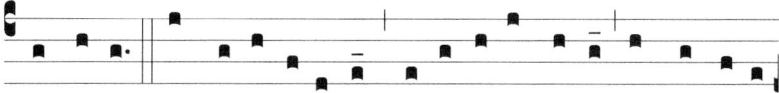

i He-væ. Ad te suspi-rámus, geméntes et flentes in hac lacri-
of Eve. *To thee do we sigh, groaning and weeping in this vale of tears.*

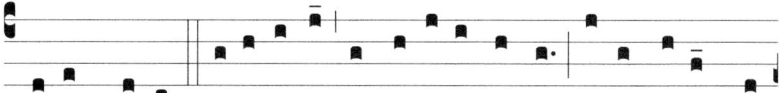

má-rum val-le. E-ia ergo, Advo-cá-ta noſtra, il-los tu- os mi-
Come then, O our Advocate, turn thou on us those merci-

se-ri-córdes ó-cu-los ad nos convér-te. Et Je-sum, be-ne-díĉtum
ful eyes of thine. *And shew unto us, after this*

fruĉtum ventris tu- i, no-bis poſt hoc exsí- li- um o-ſténde.
exile, Jesus, the blessed fruit of thy womb.

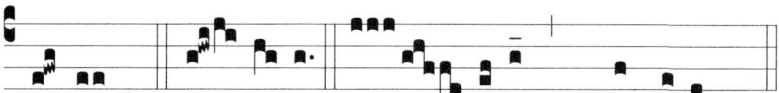

O cle- mens : O pi- a : O dulcis * Virgo Ma- rí- a.
O clement, O loving, O sweet Virgin Mary.

Solemn
I.

Sal- ve, * Re- gí- na, ma-ter mi- se-ri-córdi- æ : Vi- ta, dul-cé- do, et spes noſtra, sal- ve. Ad te cla-má- mus, éxsu-les, fí- li- i He-vae. Ad te suspi-rá- mus, ge-méntes et flen- tes in hac lacri-má-rum val-le. E- ia ergo, Advo-cá- ta noſtra, il-los tu- os mi-se-ri-cór-des ó-cu-los ad nos convér- te. Et Je-sum, be-ne-dí- ctum fructum ventris tu- i, no- bis poſt hoc exsí-li- um o- ſténde. O cle-mens : O pi- a : O dulcis * Virgo Ma-rí- a.

℣. Ora pro nobis, sancta Dei Génitrix. ℟. Ut digni efficiámur promissiónibus Christi.

Orémus.

Omnípotens sempitérne Deus, qui gloriósæ Vírginis Matris Maríæ corpus et ánimam, ut dignum Fílii tui habitáculum éffici mererétur, Spíritu Sancto cooperánte, præparásti : † da, ut cujus commemoratióne lætámur, * ejus pia intercessióne, ab instántibus malis et a morte perpétua liberémur. Per eúndem Christum Dóminum nóstrum. ℟. Amen.

℣. Pray for us, O holy Mother of God. ℟. That we may be made worthy of the promises of Christ.

Let us pray.

Almighty, everlasting God, who by the coöperation of the Holy Ghost, didst prepare the body and soul of Mary, glorious Virgin and Mother, to become a dwelling meet for Thy Son : grant that as we rejoice in her commemoration, so by her pitiful intercession we may be delivered from present evils and from everlasting death. Through the same Christ our Lord. ℟. Amen.

48

Aspersion of Holy Water.

The custom of performing the aspersion of holy water after Compline, albeit widespread, is not found in any of the liturgical books promulgated after the Council of Trent, and is therefore regulated by local use. The following antiphons may be sung *recto tono* in a low voice, kneeling except on Saturday and Sunday and during Eastertide.

¶ During the year.

Aspérges me, * Dómine hyssópo, et mundabor : lavábis me, et super nívem dealbábor. Ps. 50. Miserére mei, Deus, * secúndum magnam misericórdiam tuam. Glória Patri, et Fílio, * et Spirítui Sancto. Sicut erat in princípio, et nunc, et semper, * et in sǽcula sæculórum. Amen. Repeat : Aspérges me, &c.

Thou shalt sprinkle me, O Lord, with hyssop, and I shall be cleansed : thou shalt wash me, and I shall be made whiter than snow. Have mercy on me, O God, according to thy great mercy. Glory be to the Father, and to the Son, and to the Holy Ghost. As it was in the beginning is now, and ever shall be, world without end. Amen.

¶ During Passiontide, the ℣. Glória Patri is not said, except on feasts.

¶ In Eastertide.

Vidi aquam * egrediéntem de templo, a látere dextro, allelúia : et omnes, ad quos pervénit aqua ista, salvi facti sunt, et dicent, allelúia, allelúa. Ps. 117. Confitémini Dómino quóniam bonus : * quóniam in sǽculum misericórdia ejus. Glória Patri, et Fílio, * et Spirítui Sancto. Sicut erat in princípio, et nunc, et semper, * et in sǽcula sæculórum. Amen. Repeat : Vidi aquam, &c.

I saw water coming forth from the temple, on the right side, alleluia : and all those to whom this water came were saved, and shall say, alleluia, alleluia. Confess ye to our Lord because he is good : because his mercy is for ever. Glory be to the Father, and to the Son, and to the Holy Ghost. As it was in the beginning is now, and ever shall be, world without end. Amen.

Seasonal and Proper Festal Melodies of the Hymn.

❧ On feasts without a proper melody that fall during a season or octave with a proper one, the hymn is sung according to the setting of the respective season or octave.

❧ On feasts of Our Lady and their octaves, except the Seven Dolours.

Te lu- cis ante térmi-num, Re-rum Cre- á- tor, pó-scimus, Ut só-li-ta cle- mén-ti- a, Sis præ-sul ad cu-stó-di-am. 2. Pro-cul re- cé-dant sómni- a, Et nócti- um phantásma-ta : Hostémque nostrum cómprime, Ne pol-lu- án-tur córpo-

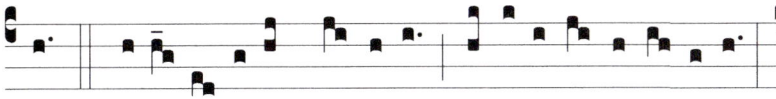

ra. 3. Gló- ri- a ti-bi,4 Dó-mi-ne, Qui na-tus es de Vír-gi-ne,
Glory be to thee, O Lord, who wast born of the Virgin, with the Fa-

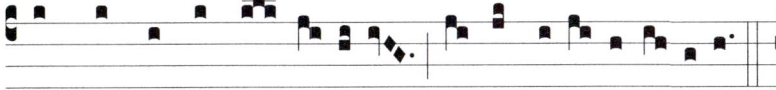

Cum Pa tre et Sancto Spí- ri-tu, In sempi- térna sǽ-cu-la.
ther and the Holy Ghost, world without end.

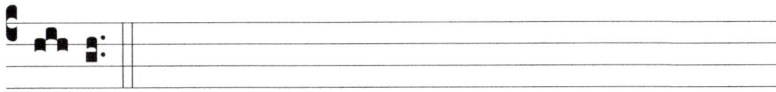

A- men.

¶ During Advent.

e lu-cis ante térmi-num, Re- rum Cre- á- tor, pósci-

mus, Ut só-li-ta cle-ménti- a, Sis præ-sul ad cu-stó-di- am.

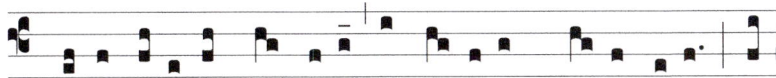

2. Pro-cul re-cé-dant sómni- a, Et nó-cti- um phantásma-ta : Ho-

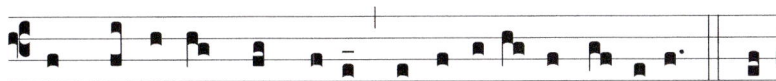

stémque nostrum cómprime, Ne pol-lu- án-tur córpo-ra. 3. Præsta, Pa-ter omní-po-tens, Per Je-sum Chri-stum Dómi-num,

Qui te-cum in perpé-tu- um, Regnat cum Sancto Spí- ri-tu.

A- men.

¶ In Christmastide.

8.

Te lu-cis ante tér-mi-num, Re- rum Cre- á-tor, pósci-mus, Ut pro tu- a cleménti- a, Sis præ-sul ad cu-stó-di- am.

2. Pro-cul re-cé-dant sóm-ni- a, Et nócti- um phantásma-ta :

Hostémque nostrum cómprime, Ne pol-lu- án- tur córpo-ra.

(music notation)

3. Gló-ri- a ti-bi, Dó- mi-ne, Qui natus es de Vír-gi-ne, Cum
Glory be to thee, O Lord, who wast born of the Virgin, with the Father

(music notation)

Pa tre et Sancto Spí- ri-tu, In sempi-tér- na sǽ-cu-la. A- men.
and the Holy Ghost, world without end.

On the feast of the Epiphany and its octave.

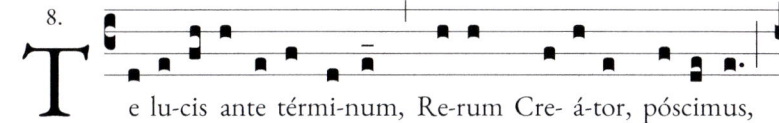

8.

(music notation)

Te lu-cis ante térmi-num, Re-rum Cre- á-tor, póscimus,

(music notation)

Ut só-li-ta cleménti- a, Sis præ-sul ad custó-di- am. 2. Pro-cul

(music notation)

re-cé-dant sómni- a, Et nócti- um phantásma-ta : Hostémque

(music notation)

nostrum cómpri-me, Ne pol-lu- ántur córpo-ra. 3. Gló-ri- a ti-
Glory be to thee,

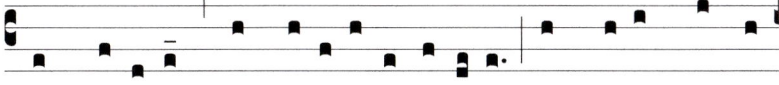

(music notation)

bi,4 Dómi-ne, Qui appá-ru- í-sti hó-di- e, Cum Patre et Sancto
O Lord, who didst appear to-day, with the Father and the Holy Ghost, world

Spí- ri- tu,   In sempi- térna sǽ-cu-la.   A- men.
without end.

¶ On the feaſt of the Holy Family, the tone is of the Epiphany with the following doxology :

3. Je-su, tu- is ob-é-di- ens Qui factus es pa-rénti-bus, Cum Patre
O Jesu, who wast obedient to thy parents, glory always be to thee, with the

su mmo ac Spí- ri- tu, Semper ti-bi sit gló-ri- a.   A- men.
Father moſt high and the Ghoſt.

¶ During Lent.

T e lu- cis ante térmi-num, Re-rum Cre- á-tor, pósci-

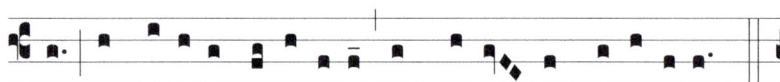

mus, Ut só-li-ta cleménti- a, Sis præ-sul   ad cuſtó-di- am.

2. Pro-cul re- cé-dant sómni- a, Et nócti- um phantásma-ta : Ho-

stémque nostrum cómprime, Ne pol-lu-   ántur córpo-ra. 3. Præ-

sta, Pa- ter omní-po-tens, Per Je-sum Chri-stum Dómi-num Qui

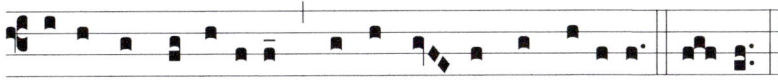

te-cum in perpé-tu- um Regnat cum Sancto Spí- ri-tu.   A- men.

¶ In Passiontide.

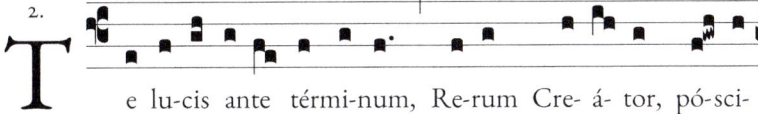

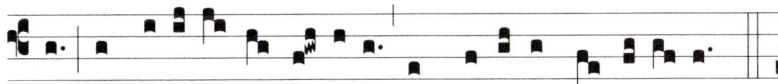

2.

T e lu-cis ante térmi-num, Re-rum Cre- á- tor, pó-sci-

mus, Ut só-li- ta cle-mén-ti- a, Sis præ-sul ad cu-stó-di- am.

2. Pro- cul re-cé-dant sómni- a,   Et nócti- um phantásma- ta :

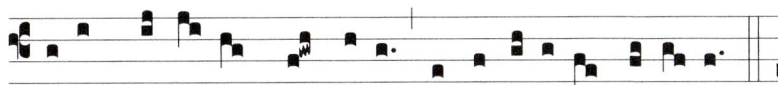

Hostémque nostrum cómprime, Ne pol-lu- ántur córpo- ra.

56

3. Præsta, Pa-ter omní-po-tens, Per Je-sum Chri-stum Dó-mi-num

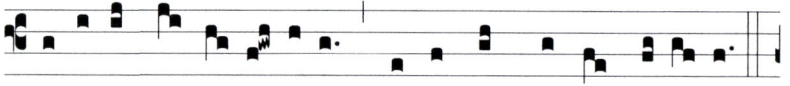

Qui te-cum in perpé- tu- um Regnat cum Sancto Spí- ri- tu.

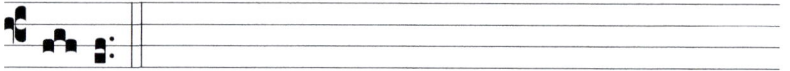

A- men.

¶ In Eastertide.

8.

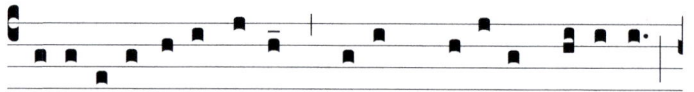

Te lu-cis ante térmi-num, Re-rum Cre- á-tor, póscimus,

Ut só- li- ta cleménti- a, Sis præ- sul ad custó-di- am.

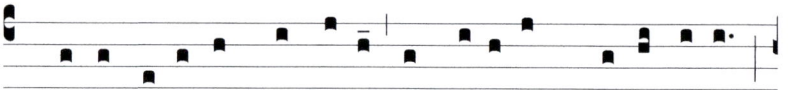

2. Pro-cul re-cé-dant sómni- a, Et nócti- um phantásma-ta :

Hostémque nostrum cómprime, Ne pol-lu- ántur córpo-ra.

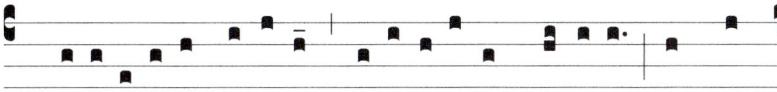

3. Gló-ri- a ti-bi, Dómi-ne, Qui surréx-í-sti a mórtu- is, Cum Pa-tre
Glory be to thee, O Lord, who hast risen from the dead, with the Father and

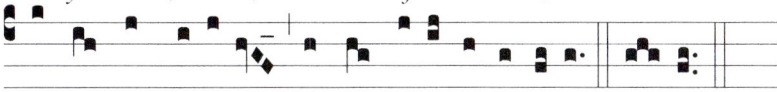

et Sancto Spí- ri-tu, In sempi- térna sǽ-cu-la. A- men.
the Holy Ghost, world without end.

❡ From the Ascension of our Lord to Pentecost exclusive.

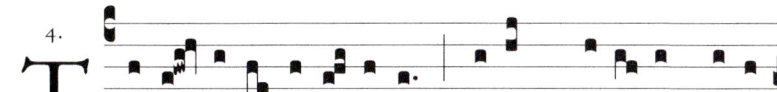

4.

T e lu- cis an-te térmi-num, Re-rum Cre- á- tor, pósci-

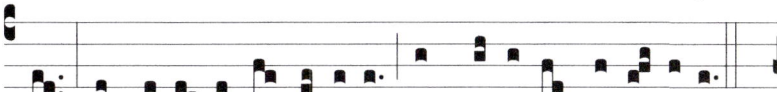

mus, Ut só-li- ta cle-ménti- a, Sis præ-sul ad custó- di- am.

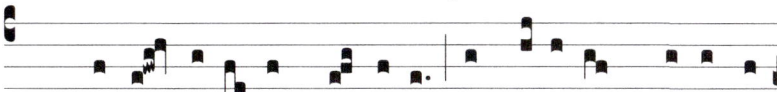

2. Pro-cul re-cé-dant sómni- a, Et nócti- um phantásma-

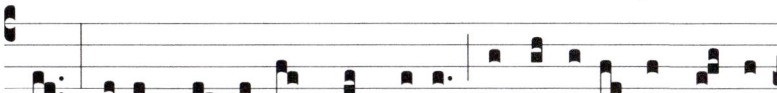

ta : Hostémque nostrum cómprime, Ne pol-lu- án-tur cór-po-

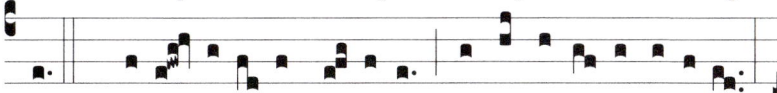

ra. 3. Gló-ri- a ti- bi, Dó-mi-ne, Qui scandis su-per sí-de- ra,
Glory be to thee, O Lord, who dost ascend above the stars, with the

Cum Pa tre et Sancto Spí- ri- tu,   In sempi- térna sǽ- cu- la.
Father and the Holy Ghost, world without end.

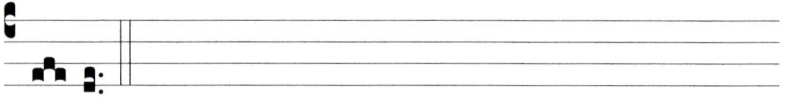

A- men.

❡ On the feast of Pentecost and its octave.

1. Te lu-cis ante térmi-num, Re- rum Cre- á- tor, póscimus,

Ut só- li- ta cle-mén- ti- a, Sis præ-sul ad cu-stó-di- am.

2. Pro-cul re-cé-dant sómni- a,   Et nócti- um phantásma-ta :

Hostémque nostrum cómpri-me, Ne pol-lu- án- tur córpo-ra.

3. Gló-ri- a Pa-tri Dómi-no Na-tóque, qui a mórtu- is Surré-
Glory be to the Lord Father and to the Son, who did rise from the dead,

xit, ac Pa-rá-cli-to, In sæ-cu-ló-rum sǽ-cu-la. A-men.

and to the Paraclete, world without end.

On the feast of Corpus Christi and its octave, the tone and doxology are those of Christmas.

On the feast of the Sacred Heart of Jesus and its octave.

3. Te lu-cis an-te térmi-num, Re-rum Cre-á-tor, pó-

sci-mus, Ut só-li-ta cle-mén-ti-a, Sis præ-sul ad custó-di-

am. 2. Pro-cul re-cé-dant sómni-a, Et nó-cti-um phantá-

sma-ta: Hostémque no-strum cómpri-me, Ne pol-lu-án-tur

cór-po-ra. 3. Gló-ri-a ti-bi, Dó-mi-ne, Qui Cor-de fundis

Glory be to thee, O Lord, who pourest forth grace from thy

60

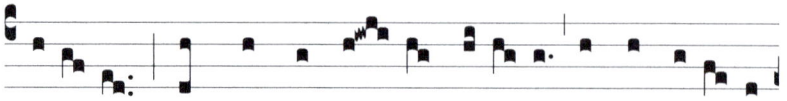

gra- ti- am, Cum Pa tre et San- &to Spí- ri- tu   In sempi- térna
heart, with the Father and the Holy Ghost, world without end.

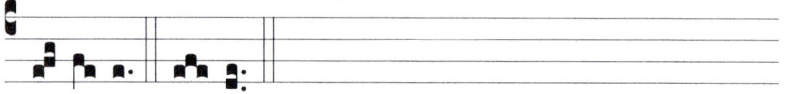

sǽ- cu- la.   A- men.

¶ On the feast of the Transfiguration of our Lord, the tone and doxology are those of Epiphany.

¶ On both feasts of the Seven Dolours of the Blessed Virgin Mary, the tone is that of Passiontide with the following doxology :

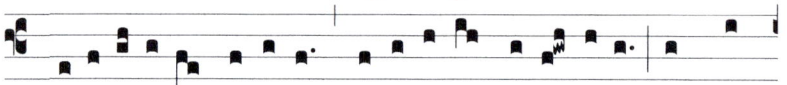

3. Gló-ri- a ti- bi, Dómi-ne, Qui passus es pro sér-vu-lis Cum Pa-tre
Glory be to thee, O Lord, who didst suffer for thy servants, with the Father

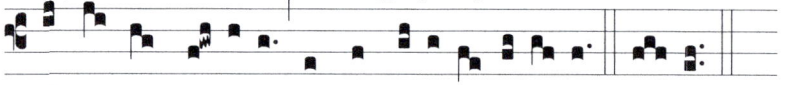

et San&to Spí- ri-tu,   In sémpi-terna sǽ-cu- la.   A- men.
and the Holy Ghost, world without end.

¶ On the feast of Christ the King.

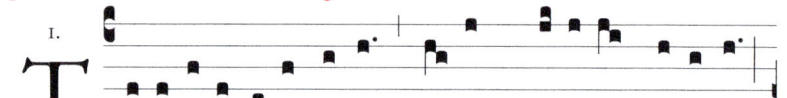

Te lu-cis ante térmi-num, Re-rum Cre- á-tor, póscimus,

Ut só-li- ta cle-mén-ti- a, Sis præ-sul ad cu-stó-di- am.

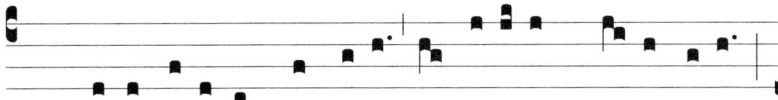

2. Pro-cul re-cé-dant sómni- a, Et nóĉti- um phantásma-ta :

Hoŝtémque noŝtrum cómpri-me, Ne pol-lu- án- tur córpo-ra.

3. Gló-ri- a ti-bi, Dómi-ne, Qui sceptra mundi témpe-ras, Cum
Glory be to thee, O Lord, who ruleŝt the kingdoms of the world, with the

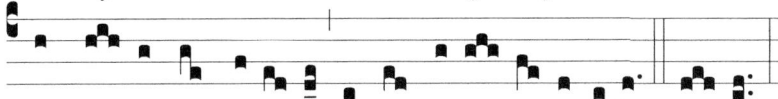

Pa tre et Sanĉto Spí- ri- tu, In sempi-tér- na sæ-cu-la. A- men.
Father and the Holy Ghoŝt, world without end.

On Maundy Thursday and Good Friday.

❡ Jube, domne, the short lesson, the ℣. Adjutórium, and Pater noster are all omitted. Compline begins with Confíteor, Misereátur, and Indulgéntiam, as on page 15. The usual psalms and the canticle are then said *recto tono* without an antiphon or Glória Patri and dropping a whole tone after the last accented syllable of each.

Psalm 4.

1. Cum invo-cá-rem exaudí-vit me De- us jus-tí- ti- æ me- æ : *

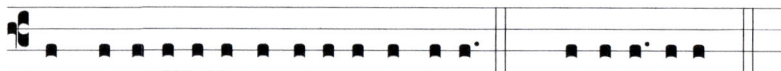

in tri-bu-la-ti- ó-ne di- la-tás-ti mi-hi. Flex : peccá-re : †

2. Miserére mei, * et exáudi oratiónem meam.

3. Fílii hóminum úsquequo gravi corde ? * ut quid dilígitis vanitátem et quǽritis mendácium ?

4. Et scitóte quóniam mirificávit Dóminus sanctum suum : * Dóminus exáudiet me cum clamávero ad eum.

5. Irascímini, et nolíte peccáre : † quæ dícitis in córdibus vestris, * in cubílibus vestris compungímini.

6. Sacrificáte sacrifícium justítiæ, † et speráte in Dómino. * Multi dicunt : quis osténdit nobis bona ?

7. Signátum est super nos lumen vultus tui, Dómine : * dedísti lætítiam in corde meo.

8. A fructu fruménti, vini et ólei sui * multiplicáti sunt.

9. In pace in idípsum * dórmiam et requiéscam.

10. Quó-ni- am tu, Dómi-ne, singu-lá-ri- ter in spe * consti-tu- í-

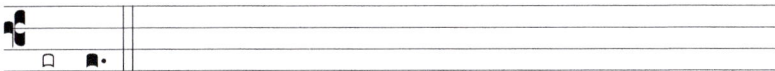

sti me.

Psalm 30.

1. In te Dómine sperávi, non confúndar in ætérnum : * in justítia tua líbera me.

2. Inclína ad me aurem tuam, * accélera ut éruas me.

3. Esto mihi in Deum protectórem, et in domum refúgii, * ut salvum me fácias.

4. Quóniam fortitúdo mea et refúgium meum es tu : * et propter nomen tuum dedúces me, et enútries me.

5. Edúces me de láqueo hoc, quem abscondérunt mihi : * quóniam tu es protéctor meus.

6. In manus tuas comméndo spíritum meum : * redemísti me Dómine Deus veritátis.

Psalm 90.

1. Qui hábitat in adjutório Altíssimi, * in protectióne Dei cæli commo-rábitur.

2. Dicet Dómino : Suscéptor meus es tu, et refúgium meum : * Deus meus sperábo in eum.

3. Quóniam ipse liberávit me de láqueo venántium, * et a verbo áspero.

4. Scápulis suis obumbrábit tibi : * et sub pennis ejus sperábis.

5. Scuto circúmdabit te véritas ejus : * non timébis a timóre noctúrno.

6. A sagítta volánte in die, † a negótio perambulánte in ténebris : * ab incúrsu et dæmónio meridiáno.

7. Cadent a látere tuo mille, † et decem míllia a dextris tuis : * ad te autem non appropinquábit.

8. Verúmtamen óculis tuis considerábis : * et retributiónem peccató-rum vidébis.

9. Quóniam tu es Dómine spes mea : * Altíssimum posuísti refúgium tuum.

10. Non accédet ad te malum : * et flagéllum non appropinquábit ta-bernáculo tuo.

11. Quóniam Angelis suis mandávit de te : * ut custódiant te in ómnibus viis tuis.

12. In mánibus portábunt te : * ne forte offéndas ad lápidem pedem tuum.

13. Super áspidem et basilíscum ambulábis : * et conculcábis leónem et dracónem.

14. Quóniam in me sperávit, liberábo eum : * prótegam eum quóniam cognóvit nomen meum.

15. Clamábit ad me, et ego exáudiam eum : † cum ipso sum in tribulatióne : * erípiam eum et glorificábo eum.

16. Longitúdine diérum replébo eum : * et osténdam illi salutáre meum.

Psalm 133.

1. Ecce nunc benedícite Dóminum, * omnes servi Dómini.

2. Qui statis in domo Dómini, * in átriis domus Dei nostri.

3. In nóctibus extóllite manus vestras in sancta, * et benedícite Dóminum.

4. Benedícat te Dóminus ex Sion, * qui fecit cælum et terram.

Canticle of Simeon (Luke 2. e).

1. Nunc dimíttis servum tuum, Dómine, * secúndum verbum tuum in pace :

2. Quia vidérunt óculi mei * salutáre tuum :

3. Quod parásti * ante fáciem ómnium populórum :

4. Lumen ad revelatiónem Géntium, * et glóriam plebis tuæ Israel.

66

¶ Then all kneel and say the following antiphon *recto tono* :

Ant. Christus * factus est pro nobis obédiens usque ad mortem.

Ant. Christ became obedient for us unto death.

¶ On Good Friday is added :

Mortem autem crucis.

Even to the death of the cross.

¶ Then Pater noster is said entirely in silence, and afterwards the following psalm is sung *recto tono* but a little higher than before, with a drop of a whole tone after the last accented syllable :

Psalm 50.

1. Miserére mei Deus, * secúndum magnam misericórdiam tuam.

1. Have mercy on me, O God, according to thy great mercy.

2. Et secúndum multitúdinem miseratiónum tuárum, * dele iniquitátem meam.

2. And according to the multitude of thy commiserations, take away mine iniquity.

3. Amplius lava me ab iniquitáte mea : * et a peccáto meo munda me.

3. Wash me more amply from mine iniquity : and cleanse me from my sin.

4. Quóniam iniquitátem meam ego cognósco : * et peccátum meum contra me est semper.

4. Because I do know mine iniquity : and my sin is before me always.

5. Tibi soli peccávi, et malum coram te feci : * ut justificéris in sermónibus tuis, et vincas cum judicáris.

5. To thee only have I sinned, and have done evil before thee : that thou mayst be justified in thy word, and mayst overcome when thou art judged.

6. Ecce enim in iniquitátibus concéptus sum : * et in peccátis concépit me mater mea.

7. Ecce enim veritátem dilexísti : * incérta et occúlta sapiéntiæ tuæ manifestásti mihi.

8. Aspérges me hyssópo, et mundábor : * lavábis me, et super nivem dealbábor.

9. Audítui meo dabis gáudium et lætítiam : * et exsultábunt ossa humiliáta.

10. Avérte fáciem tuam a peccátis meis : * et omnes iniquitátes meas dele.

11. Cor mundum crea in me Deus : * et spíritum rectum ínnova in viscéribus meis.

12. Ne projícias me a fácie tua : * et spíritum sanctum tuum ne áuferas a me.

13. Redde mihi lætítiam salutáris tui : * et spíritu principáli confírma me.

6. For behold I was conceived in iniquities : and my mother conceived in sins.

7. For behold thou hast loved truth : the uncertain and hidden things of thy wisdom thou hast made manifest to me.

8. Thou shalt sprinkle me with hyssop, and I shall be cleansed : thou shalt wash me, and I shall be made whiter than snow.

9. To my hearing thou shalt give joy and gladness : and the humbled bones shall rejoice.

10. Turn away thy face from my sins : and wipe away all mine iniquities.

11. Create a clean heart in me, O God : and renew a right spirit within my bowels.

12. Cast me not away from thy face : and thy holy spirit take not from me.

13. Render unto me the joy of thy salvation : and confirm me with the principal spirit.

68

14. Docébo iníquos vias tuas : * et ímpii ad te converténtur.

15. Líbera me de sanguínibus Deus, Deus salútis meæ : * et exsultábit lingua mea justítiam tuam.

16. Dómine lábia mea apéries : * et os meum annuntiábit laudem tuam.

17. Quóniam si voluísses sacrifícium, dedíssem útique : * holocáustis non delectáberis.

18. Sacrifícium Deo spíritus contribulátus : * cor contrítum, et humiliátum, Deus, non despícies.

19. Benígne fac Dómine in bona voluntáte tua Sion : * ut ædificéntur muri Jerúsalem.

20. Tunc acceptábis sacrifícium justítiæ, oblatiónes, et holocáusta : * tunc impónent super altáre tuum vítulos.

14. I will teach the unjust thy ways : and the impious shall be converted to thee.

15. Deliver me from bloods, O God, the God of my salvation : and my tongue shall exult for thy justice.

16. Lord, thou wilt open my lips : and my mouth shall shew forth thy praise.

17. Because if thou wouldest have had sacrifice, I had verily given it : with holocausts thou wilt not be delighted.

18. A sacrifice to God is an afflicted spirit : a contrite and humbled heart, O God, thou wilt not despise.

19. Deal favourably, O Lord, in thy good will with Sion : that the walls of Jerusalem may be built up.

20. Then shalt thou accept the sacrifice of justice, oblations, and holocausts : then shall they lay calves upon thine altar.

¶ The Officiant concludes the Office saying the following collect in the same tone as the psalm and likewise dropping a whole tone on the last syllable :

Réspice, quæsumus Dómine, super hanc famíliam tuam, pro qua Dóminus noster Jesus Christus non dubitávit mánibus tradi nocéntium, et crucis subíre torméntum. And in silence : Qui tecum vivit et regnat in unitáte Spíritus Sancti, Deus, per ómnia sæcula sæculórum.

Look down, we beseech thee, O Lord, on this thy family, for which our Lord Jesus Christ did not hesitate to be delivered up into the hands of wicked men, and to suffer the torment of the Cross. Who with thee liveth and reigneth, in the unity of the Holy Ghost, one God, world without end.

On Holy Saturday.

¶ Jube, domne, the short lesson, the ℣. Adjutórium, Pater noſter, Confíteor, Misereátur, Indulgéntiam, the ℣. Convérte nos, and the ℣. Deus in adjutórium are all said as usual with Allelúia, as on page 13. Then the usual psalms are sung without an antiphon in the following tone :

Psalm 4.

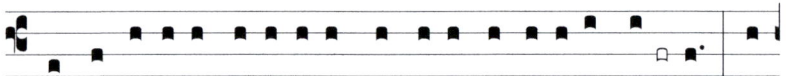

1. *Cum in*vo-cá-rem exaudí-vit me De- us jus-tí- ti- *æ* me-   æ : * in

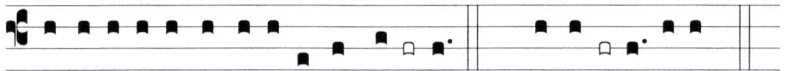

tri-bu-la-ti- ó-ne di-la-*tás-ti* mi-   hi. Flex : pec*cá-re* : †

2. Miser*ére* mei, * et exáudi orati*ónem* meam.

3. Fílii hóminum úsquequo gra*vi* corde ? * ut quid dilígitis vanitátem et quǽri*tis men*dácium ?

4. Et scitóte quóniam mirificávit Dóminus sanc*tum* <u>su</u>um : * Dóminus exáudiet me cum clamáve*ro ad* <u>e</u>um.

5. Irascímini, et nolíte pecc<u>á</u>re : † quæ dícitis in córdi*bus* <u>ve</u>stris, * in cubílibus veſtris *compungí*mini.

6. Sacrificáte sacrifícium juſt<u>í</u>tiæ, † et speráte *in* <u>Dó</u>mino. * Multi dicunt: quis oſténdit *nobis* <u>bo</u>na ?

7. Signátum eſt super nos lumen vultus tu*i*, <u>Dó</u>mine : * dedíſti lætítiam in *corde* <u>me</u>o.

8. A fruĉtu fruménti, vini et óle*i* <u>su</u>i * mul*tiplic*<u>á</u>ti sunt.

9. In pace in *idíp*<u>s</u>um * dórmiam et *requi*<u>é</u>scam.

10. Quóniam tu Dómine singulári*ter* <u>in</u> spe * con*ſtituí*sti me.

11. Glória Patri, *et* <u>Fí</u>lio, * et Spirí*tui* <u>Sanĉ</u>to.

12. Sicut erat in princípio, et nunc, *et* <u>sem</u>per, * et in sǽcula sæcu*lórum*. <u>A</u>men.

Psalm 30.

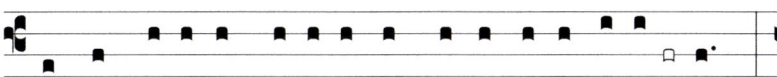

1. *In te,* Dómi-ne, spe-rá-vi non confúndar in æ-<u>tér</u>- num : *

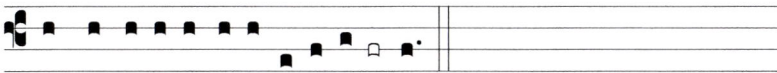

in jus-tí- ti- a tu- a *lí-be-*<u>ra</u> me.

2. Inclína ad me au*rem* <u>tu</u>am, * accélera ut *é*ru<u>as</u> me.

3. Eſto mihi in Deum proteĉtórem, et in domum *refú*gii, * ut sal*vum me* <u>fá</u>cias.

4. Quóniam fortitúdo mea et refúgium me*um* es tu : * et propter no-men tuum dedúces me, et e*nútri*es me.

5. Edúces me de láqueo hoc, quem abscondé*runt* mihi : * quóniam tu es pro*téctor* meus.

6. In manus tuas comméndo spíri*tum* meum : * redemísti me Dómine Deus *veri*tátis.

7. Glória Patri, *et* Fílio, * et Spirí*tui* Sanĉto.

8. Sicut erat in princípio, et nunc, *et* semper, * et in sǽcula sæcu*lórum*. Amen.

Psalm 90.

1. *Qui há*-bi- tat in adju-tó-ri- o *Altís*-simi, * in pro-tec-ti- ó-ne

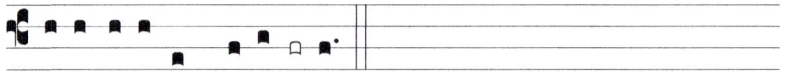

De- i cæ-li *commo*-rá-bi-tur.

2. Dicet Dómino: Suscéptor meus es tu, et refúgi*um* meum : * Deus meus sperá*bo in* eum.

3. Quóniam ipse liberávit me de láqueo *venán*tium, * et a *verbo* áspero.

4. Scápulis suis obumbrá*bit* tibi : * et sub pennis e*jus ſpe*rábis.

5. Scuto circúmdabit te véri*tas* ejus : * non timébis a timó*re noc*túrno.

6. A sagítta volánte in die, † a negótio perambulánte *in* ténebris : * ab incúrsu et dæmónio me*ridi*áno.

7. Cadent a látere tuo mille, † et decem míllia a dex*tris* tuis : * ad te autem non ap*propin*quábit.

8. Verúmtamen óculis tuis consi*derá*bis : * et retributiónem peccató-
*rum vi*débis.

9. Quóniam tu es Dómine *spes* mea : * Altíssimum posuísti refú*gium*
tuum.

10. Non accédet ad *te* malum : * et flagéllum non appropinquábit ta-
bern*áculo* tuo.

11. Quóniam Angelis suis mandá*vit* de te : * ut custódiant te in ómnibus
viis tuis.

12. In mánibus *por*tábunt te : * ne forte offéndas ad lápidem *pedem*
tuum.

13. Super áspidem et basilíscum am*bu*lábis : * et conculcábis leónem *et*
*dra*cónem.

14. Quóniam in me sperávit, libera*bo* eum : * prótegam eum quóniam
cognóvit *nomen* meum.

15. Clamábit ad me, et ego exáudiam eum : † cum ipso sum in tribula-
*ti*óne : * erípiam eum et glorifi*cábo* eum.

16. Longitúdine diérum replé*bo* eum : * et osténdam illi salu*táre* meum.

17. Glória Patri, *et* Fílio, * et Spirí*tui* Sancto.

18. Sicut erat in princípio, et nunc, *et* semper, * et in sǽcula sæcu*lórum*.
Amen.

Psalm 133.

1. *Ecce* nunc be-ne-dí-ci-*te* Dómi-num, * omnes *servi* Dómi-ni :

2. Qui statis in do*mo* Dómini, * in átriis domus *Dei* nostri.

3. In nóctibus extóllite manus vestras *in* san̆cta, * et benedí*cite* Dóminum.

4. Benedícat te Dóminus *ex* Sion, * qui fecit cæ*lum et* terram.

5. Glória Patri, *et* Fílio, * et Spirí*tui* San̆cto.

6. Sicut erat in princípio, et nunc, *et* semper, * et in sǽcula sæcu*lórum.* Amen.

¶ The hymn Te lucis, the chapter, the short ℟. In manus, and the ℣. Custódi are all omitted.

Ant.
8. G

Vé-spe-re au-tem sábba-ti.

Canticle of Simeon (Luke 2. e).

1. *Nunc di*mít-tis servum tu- um Dómi-ne, * se-cúndum verbum

tu-*um in* pa- ce : 2. *Qui- a* vi-dé-runt *&c.* 3. Quod pa-rá-sti *

2. *Quia* vidérunt óculi mei * salu*táre* tuum :

3. Quod parásti * ante fáciem ómnium *populó*rum :

4. *Lumen* ad revelatiónem Géntium, * et glóriam plebis *tuæ* Israel.

5. *Glória* Patri, et Fílio, * et Spirí*tui* San̆cto.

6. *Sicut* erat in princípio, et nunc et semper, * et in sǽcula sæcu*lórum.* Amen.

Ant.

V e-spe-re au-tem sábba-ti, quæ lu-céscit in prima sábba-

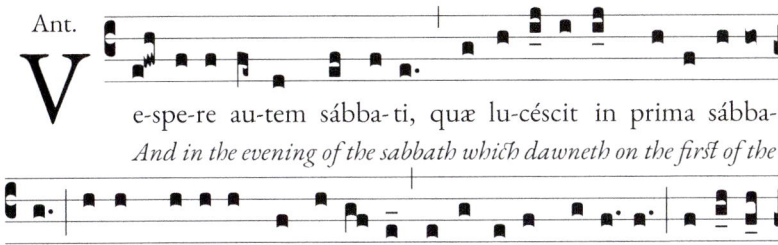

And in the evening of the sabbath which dawneth on the first of the

ti, ve-nit Ma-rí- a Magda- lé-ne, et ál-te-ra Ma-rí- a, vi-dé-re

sabbath, came Mary Magdalen and the other Mary to see the sepulchre.

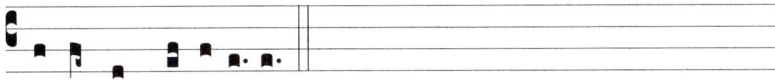

se-púlcrum, al-le-lú- ia.

¶ The Officiant then immediately says the ℣. Dóminus vobíscum and the collect Vísita, quǽsumus, with all that usually follows, as on page 36.

During the Octave of Easter.

¶ Jube, domne, the short lesson, the ℣. Adjutórium, Pater noster, Confíteor, Misereátur, Indulgéntiam, the ℣. Convérte nos, and the ℣. Deus in adjutórium are all said as usual with Allelúia, as on page 13. Then the usual psalms are sung in tone 8. G, as on page 62, after which the following antiphon is sung :

Ant.
8.

A l- le-lú-ia, al-le-lú- ia, al-le-lú-ia, al-le-lú- ia.

¶ The hymn Te lucis, the chapter, the short ℟. In manus, and the ℣. Custódi are all omitted. The usual canticle is sung in the following tone :

Canticle of Simeon (Luke 2. e).

1. *Nunc di*mít-tis servum tu- *um*, Dómi-ne, * se-cúndum verbum

tu- *um in* pa- ce : 2. *Qui- a* vi-dé-runt *&c.* 3. Quod pa-rá-sti *

2. *Quia* vidérunt ócu*li* mei * salu*táre* tuum :

3. Quod *parásti* * ante fáciem ómnium *populórum* :

4. *Lumen* ad revelatió*nem* Géntium, * et glóriam plebis *tuæ* Israel.

5. *Glóri*a Patri, *et* Fílio, * et Spirí*tui* Sancto.

6. *Sicut* erat in princípio, et nunc, *et* semper, * et in sæcula sæcu*lórum*. Amen.

¶ After the canticle the following antiphon is sung :

Ant. 2.

Hæc di- es, * quam fe- cit
This is the day which the Lord hath made :

Dó- mi- nus : exsul-té- mus,
let us be glad and rejoice therein.

et læ- té- mur in e- a.

¶ The Officiant then immediately says the ℣. Dóminus vobíscum and the collect Vísita, quǽsumus, with all that usually follows, as on page 36.

¶ Compline of Saturday *in Albis* is said according to the usual order, as on p. 13.

✠

Laus Deo

Printed in Dunstable, United Kingdom